BESS
~OF~
HARDWICK
(in simple terms)

Alison Ratcliffe-Williams

AuthorHouse™ UK
1663 Liberty Drive
Bloomington, IN 47403 USA
www.authorhouse.co.uk
UK TFN: 0800 0148641 (Toll Free inside the UK)
UK Local: 02036 956322 (+44 20 3695 6322 from outside the UK)

Front and back cover designed and illustrated by Author.

This book is printed on acid-free paper.

ISBN: 978-1-6655-9147-8 (sc)
ISBN: 978-1-6655-9146-1 (e)

Library of Congress Control Number: 2021914978

Print information available on the last page.

Published by AuthorHouse 07/23/2021

authorHOUSE®

To my Parents, who are and always have unknowingly been my inspiration.

With heartfelt thanks and respect to Sonia and Rose for seeing my potential and giving me the opportunity of working in such a beautiful, outstanding place.

To Ken for your warm welcome on my first day, sharing your knowledge, advice, continued inspiration, support and friendship.

Preface

This book is not a large book about Bess of Hardwick, although a few have been written. My aim is a short, to the point, informative book to intrigue readers into maybe wanting to find out more about Bess of Hardwick in more depth by visiting her significant Elizabethan built home namely Hardwick Hall in Derbyshire, now owned by the National Trust. Or if the reader simply wants a reference to Bess that was simple and easy to follow. I did not want to go into more detail about Bess or tell the many stories about her life but wanted to keep the book 'in simple terms' to whet the appetite of any intellectual level of reader.

I was inspired to write this book, as part of my 'in simple terms' collection, mainly by visitors and volunteer colleagues alike over the last 5 years at Hardwick Hall who wanted a short, simple to follow book with some main points of interest relating to Bess, without having to delve into larger books and/or larger references.

This is book 1 of 11 of my 'in simple terms' collection which are, in no particular order, as follows:

Bess of Hardwick.

Lady Arbella Stuart.

The Earls of Devonshire 1-4.

The Dukes of Devonshire 1-12.

The Dowager Duchess Evelyn Cavendish - The Last Resident of Hardwick Hall.

Hardwick Hall (outside).

Hardwick Hall (inside).

Hardwick Hall (contents).

Queen Elizabeth I.

Mary Queen of Scots.

The Bess of Hardwick Children.

Introduction

Bess of Hardwick was a formidable woman of the 1500's, in fact at one point she was the second most powerful, richest woman in England behind Queen Elizabeth I, who was Bess's best friend and confidant for many years.

Often Bess is not well known in our history. This book follows Bess throughout her 4 marriages. Each marriage resulting in her climbing further up the social ladder, ending with Bess being of Countess status. Each marriage provided more wealth and power for Bess. Hence the reason for Hardwick New Hall, as it is also known, being built in the late 1500's.

Hardwick Hall is a significant Elizabethan built house still with original features, a palace fit for a Princess namely Bess's granddaughter Lady Arbella Stuart, who, at that time, was a possible heir to the English throne. Hardwick Hall, now owned by the National Trust, housing the famous internationally renowned original set of Gideon tapestries dated 1578, has also one of the largest collections of original embroideries in Europe and some of the most important pieces of 16th Century furniture in Britain. Hardwick Hall has also always had pictures and portraits and has the oldest collection in the British Isles, apart from parts of the Royal Collection.

'Hardwick Hall, more glass than wall', was such a grand house when it was built with its huge many diamond shaped glass leaded windows that it inspired this very saying.

This book follows Bess from early childhood whilst giving a brief insight into her heritage through to her death.

Contents

About The Hardwicks

The Hardwicks arrived in Derbyshire from Sussex by the mid-13th Century and farmed land granted by Lord of the Manor Slingsby, Robert Savage on the North-East border of Derbyshire, overlooking Nottinghamshire.

By the mid-15th Century, the family had risen to 'Gentleman-Yeoman' stock, the lowest rank of English gentry, standing below an Esquire but above a Yeoman.

- Esquire – young nobleman in training for a Knighthood, acted as an attendant to a Knight;
- Yeoman – a man holding and cultivating a small landed estate;

The Hardwicks had estates of a few hundred acres mainly in the Parish of Ault Hucknall in the Manor of Slingsby.

The Hardwick family were members of minor gentry. Their coat-of-arms was probably granted {c.1450} to William Hardwick.

The Hardwick name means English (Yorkshire): habitational name from any one of numerous places, for example South Yorkshire or Derbyshire.

When giving evidence of his coat-of-arms in 1569, Bess's only brother James {1525-1580/81} provided heralds with a pedigree of his family, which began with a man named William who died in c.1453.

James was the last surviving legitimate male member of the Hardwick family. No male member rose above the status of Esquire or held important Local or County offices.

Bess of Hardwick

Bess of Hardwick, born Elizabeth Hardwick, was born on 27th July 1527, this year was according to many but later evidence shows her birth could have been October 1521 or February 1522, Bess's exact birth is unknown simply as she was a girl, therefore seen as not important enough to have a birth certificate, as was any girl of that era who was not born in to royalty.

Saying that, 1527 date is the most likely one, as according to Bess's witness statement under oath at a Court hearing in October 1546, she gave her age at the time of her first marriage in May 1543 as being 'of tender years', in other words less than 16 years. I will be using this year for Bess's rough age throughout this book.

Bess was born at Hardwick Manor where the Hardwick family had been living for 200 years.

Bess, who was a very distant descendant of Edward I on her father's side, was a Gentlewoman (a woman of noble birth or good social standing).

Her father John Hardwick died when she was an infant, her mother Elizabeth Leeke remarried.

Her step-father was imprisoned for debt when Bess was about 10 years old, so the family lived in genteel poverty (trying to keep the style of high social class but with little money).

At around 12/13 years old, Bess was sent to be a Lady-in-Waiting to her distant relation Anne Gainsford, Lady Zouche. This was the standard way in which well-born girls, as well as boys, were introduced to influential people who could help them rise in the world and to be introduced to potential mates. Bess is a very good example of how effective this system could be.

Both Lady Zouche and her husband George, had been in the household of Anne Boleyn, in fact Lady Zouche served Jane Seymour after Boleyn's death in 1536.

Around 1540 Sir George became Gentleman Pensioner to Henry VIII, which meant George was in Henry's elite group of attendants, similar to a bodyguard as he was never far from the King both in London and on the King's progress during the Summer.

It was very likely Bess was in London and around the Court of Henry VIII during some very interesting times.

Bess of Hardwick died at 5pm on Saturday 13th February 1608, aged approximately 81 years. She died one of the wealthiest and influential women in England during these times.

On 16th February 1608 her body was placed in a vault in All Saints Parish Church, Derby (now known as Derby Cathedral) where you can still see a memorial for Bess to this date.

Stories of her body lying in State for weeks in the Great Chamber at Hardwick Hall are a myth, a widely held but false belief.

Robert Barlow {1st marriage}

At the age of around 15 years Bess met and married her distant relative Robert Barlow, or Barley. We aren't sure when or where the nuptials took place, or even the groom's last name! He was either Barlow or Barley depending on your source, although we do know he was aged about 13 years at the time.

We know Robert was a 'sickly young man', Bess could possibly have got closer to him by helping to nurse him, the traditional story is that Robert was also said to be in employ with the household of the Zouche family. Although this story is based on oral history, which can only be dated to the late seventeenth century, which was about eighty years after Bess's death. Robert was also heir to a neighbouring estate.

The exact date of marriage in unknown but it is thought that it took place in late May 1543, shortly before the death of Robert's father on 28th May, although there is no documentary evidence to confirm this. There is also no evidence of Bess and Robert living as man and wife.

Robert died the following year on 24th December 1544. Bess's 'widow's dower' was 1/3 of the income of the Barlow properties. This gave her a 30 pound a year income, very respectable, to say a maid servant's annual pay was 3 pound a year.

Although following Robert's death, rights to the marriage were disputed. Bess was at first refused dower by Peter Freschevile (guardian to Robert's younger brother George).

A Court battle ensued, which took several years to finalise after Robert's death, resulting in Bess being awarded her claim on the Barlow Estate, plus compensation.

There is hardly any information to be found about Robert Barlow, or his family.

William Cavendish {2nd marriage}

Around the year 1545 aged 18/19 years Bess joined the service of the Marchioness of Dorset, Frances Brandon Grey, who was the daughter of Henry VIII's sister Mary Tudor and her second husband Charles Brandon, Duke of Suffolk.

Bess became close to Frances's children, Lady Jane Grey and her younger sisters Catherine and Mary.

It was probably here, through the Grey's, that Bess met her second husband Sir William Cavendish. He was twice widowed, had 10 children and was about 20 years her senior, he was a Politician, Knight and Courtier and already wealthy. His wealth was largely as a result of his work in the nuts and bolts matters of the

Dissolution of Monasteries. He was Treasurer to the King's Chamber and therefore able to select a choice of properties for himself.

They married on 20th August 1547 at 2am, at the home of the Grey family, friends of them both.

Through this marriage Bess was entitled to be called Lady Cavendish, obviously taking her up a few rungs of the ladder of Society. Sir William was well connected at the Courts of both Henry VIII and Edward VI.

During their 10-year marriage Bess and William had 8 children, with 6 surviving infancy.

During their marriage Bess and William purchased the Chatsworth estates in Derbyshire from her step-father, this was done due to possibly acting on Bess's advice for William to sell his lands in the South of England.

They then began building the palatial Chatsworth House, intending it to be the family seat of their descendants, which today still continues.

Sir William died 25th October 1557, leaving Bess a very wealthy and still young widow, although William was deep in debt to the Crown at his death, (he was accused of embezzlement from the Crown, which some people say worried him that much, the worry caused his death – better than having his head chopped off for treason I'd say).

Bess claimed the sum of his property, having insisted that his land be settled on their heirs. She had 6 of her own children plus 10 step-children at this point, although most of her step-children were married and therefore, she was not responsible for their well-being.

William St. Loe {3rd marriage}

Bess's third marriage was to Sir William St. Loe and came not long after Elizabeth I succeeded the throne in 1558.

Queen Elizbeth chose Bess's wedding date 27th August 1559 at 2am, the Queen may well have been at the wedding. Bess now held the title Lady St. Loe.

Queen Elizabeth had made Sir William the Captain of her Yeoman Guards as he had been in charge of her security for many years, he was also Chief Butler of England. Sir William had likely risked his life on her behalf during the unsuccessful rebellion of Wyatt in 1554 by carrying Elizabeth's message to Thomas Wyatt that she would go along with his plan to put herself on the throne in place of her sister Mary.

Due to his relationship with Queen Elizabeth I, William St. Loe was able to reduce the debt Bess owed from her second marriage and paid it back in full on her behalf. Maybe out of gratitude to Sir William or because Bess had been a very close friend to Elizabeth for many years, the Queen made Bess one of her Ladies of the Bedchamber (a female personal assistant and trusted confidante), a role she held for many years.

Sir William died 6 years after marrying Bess, possibly poisoned by his own brother, even William's own mother had her doubts and had accused her second son of this. If it wasn't for one of Bess's children getting sick in Derbyshire and some house matters that needed her attention, Bess returned from London to Chatsworth to look after these issues, Bess could have been fatally poisoned too by her brother-in-law, as she had become ill in London, but when Bess returned to Derbyshire, she soon regained her health.

Three weeks after she left to be in Derbyshire Sir William's brother visited their London home and within 3 days Sir William had died of suspected poisoning.

When Sir William died without male issue, his Will left everything to Bess. His brother was not happy, he thought he would be named his brother's heir.

In those days it was unusual for a wealthy man to leave all his Estate to a wife who had already been married and had children not belonging to himself. Sir William adored Bess and loved her very much, in fact, he had told her he would take care of her children if she should die first, which was very unusual indeed, by doing this he was proving his love for her. Some people say that he was also the love of Bess's life too.

Bess was now mistress of many valuable properties, had a very substantial income and could have lived comfortably for the rest of her life.

Bess had 6 children of her own and was responsible for 10 step-children from her second marriage and now 2 more step-daughters from William St. Loe, although St. Loe's daughters were now adults and otherwise provided for. Bess was now one of the wealthiest women in England. Her annual income was calculated to amount to around sixty thousand pounds, which is equivalent to approximately nineteen million pounds (in 2019's UK money value).

Bess was still a Lady of the Bedchamber with daily access to the Queen, whose favour she enjoyed. Now in her late 30's Bess had retained her looks and good health and a number of important men began courting her. Bess was not done marrying yet!

George Talbot {4th marriage}

Bess returned to Court and after considering many suitors, she chose George Talbot as her 4th husband, he was the 6th Earl of Shrewsbury and the richest man in England. They were married in 1568.

This marriage took Bess to the peak of Society, as Talbot was not only enormously wealthy but the highest-ranking nobleman in England. Bess now became the Countess of Shrewsbury.

Talbot had 7 children who were about the same age as Bess's own children. Their marriage was part of a grand dynastic alliance that secured the property of both families for future generations.

On 9th February 1568, within days of Bess marrying Talbot, there was another double ceremony. Talbot's 16-year-old son Gilbert married Bess's 12-year-old daughter Mary and also Talbot's 8-year-old daughter Grace was married to Bess's 17-year-old son Henry.

It was not uncommon for girls in Noble families to be married so young. The marriages were not consummated until the girls were much older. In fact, Henry was sent abroad for a few years to 'become a man' until Grace was 'of age', this is where Henry found his way for the rest of his life with womanising and gambling, which is another story in itself!

Bess's marriage to the Earl of Shrewsbury was her longest, it was also her unhappiest.

At first all was well, in fact, Bess handed over most of her fortune to Talbot on the understanding that he would take care of her and her children and if any of Bess's daughters married, he would take care of paying their dowry, the latter part mostly did not happen.

Soon into their marriage Talbot and Bess became Caretakers of Mary Queen of Scots. Mary had escaped captivity in Scotland, and fled south towards England, seeking the protection of her cousin, Queen Elizabeth I. It was an honour that Queen Elizabeth trusted the Shrewsbury's with such an important duty, however, Queen Elizabeth did not provide nowhere near enough money to support Mary's large retinue (entourage), Mary had roughly 100 people serving in her entourage, this was reduced to about 30 at one point but then later increased again to about 40 in Mary's latter years.

Talbot and Bess had expected this to be a temporary arrangement, in fact at first Bess was Mary's companion, working with each other on textile projects. However, the situation dragged on for about 15 years and Mary's presence in their homes, as well as the massive financial costs, political tensions, travel restrictions and living arrangements for Talbot and Bess all contributed to the utter destruction of their marriage.

The Shrewsbury's had been apart on and off since about 1580. Mary had obviously played them off one against the other. Even Queen Elizabeth tried to reconcile them – have you heard the term 'taming of the shrew?' Well, some reports over time say this saying relates to the Shrewsbury's, when Queen Elizabeth stepped in telling them they were making an embarrassment of her with their squabbling and they needed to sort themselves out.

The final straw came when Talbot found out it was likely Bess herself who started rumours that her husband and Mary had been in a relationship – any relationship between Talbot and Mary have neither been proved or disproved, but seems unlikely though given Talbot's disposition and increasingly poor health at the time.

Bess was forced out of Chatsworth House, where she was living at the time with Talbot and some of her children, who by this time were all adults and also her young granddaughter Arbella, under the watchful eyes of 40 armed guards, (although Bess classed Chatsworth as her home as she had built it with her second husband Cavendish, it was in fact officially owned by her son Henry under the law of inheritance, Henry being the eldest son from her second marriage to Cavendish).

Henry, Bess's eldest son sided with his step-father, possibly thinking Talbot would stay with him at Chatsworth and pay most of his gambling debts off. However, Talbot in fact returned to Sheffield Castle to live out the rest of his days.

Bess together with Arbella and with the help of her second and favourite son William, ended up living back at her birth place, known as Hardwick Old Hall, after purchasing it from her brother, where she subsequently started extending and building on to that property.

Talbot died on 18th November 1590. He was buried in the Shrewsbury Chapel at Sheffield Parish Church (now known as Sheffield Cathedral), where a large monument erected for Talbot can still be seen to this day.

Bess now became Dowager Countess of Shrewsbury as they were never divorced.

Although most of Talbot's possessions from Sheffield Castle were not recovered, as his then Mistress and head Housekeeper Eleanor Britton after his death fled with most of his possessions. Bess was now one of the wealthiest and influential women in England.

Within four weeks of Talbot's death, Bess started building a new house on the Hardwick Estate, in fact within yards of the house she was living in.

Bess's new house was to be known as Hardwick New Hall and was deliberately built upon on a hill. On completion no one would have any doubts who the House belonged to as for miles around, North, South, East or West, there were six rooftop tower turrets built, each with a balustrade, on which massive sculptures of two letters appear namely 'ES' on each turret.

Elizabeth Shrewsbury had at last made her mark.

Children Of Bess - Timeline

Frances Cavendish (18/6/1548-Jan.1632) age 84 years.

*Married Sir Henry Pierrepoint MP.

Had 3 children.

Temperance Cavendish (10/6/1549-1550) age 1year.

*Died in infancy.

Henry Cavendish (17/12/1550-28/10/1616) age 66 years.

*Godson of Queen Elizabeth I.

Despised his wife.

Had 8 children, 4 boys, 4 girls all illegitimate.

He was disinherited from Bess.

Bess referred to him as 'her bad son Henry'.

William Cavendish (27/12/1551?2-3/3/1626) age 74 or 75 years.

*1st Earl of Devonshire.

Had 1 child.

Favourite son of Bess.

Charles Cavendish (28/11/1553-4/4/1617) age 64 years.

*Godson of Queen May I of England.

Married Catherine Ogle (2nd wife).

Had 2 sons.

Until 1590's spent much time at Court, frequently

sending his mother news and gossip.

Elizabeth Cavendish (31/3/1555-21/1/1582) age 27 years.

*Wife of Charles Stuart, 1st Earl of Lennox.

One daughter, Arbella, 2nd Countess of Lennox.

Mary Cavendish (Jan.1556-Apr.1632) aged 76 years.

*Married Gilbert Talbot.

Had 5 children.

Lucrece Cavendish (born and died 1556)

*Probably twin of Mary.

Supplementary Information

Bess's careful planning of her children's marriages was very successful.

She is the ancestor of many of the Noble families of today's Britain, including –

The Dukedoms of Devonshire, Norfolk, Portland, Somerset and Newcastle.

The Earls of Lincoln, Portsmouth, Kellie and Pembroke.

In fact, only in death did Bess get her lineage to the English throne, she is, most grandly, a 10 times great-grandmother to the current Queen Elizabeth II of England and the current Princes' William and Harry are descended from Bess on both sides.

Georgiana, who married the 5th Duke of Devonshire, was also a descendant of Diana, Princess of Wales (mother to Princes' William and Harry) Georgiana being a Spencer.

His Grace, The Duke of Devonshire Peregrine Andrew Morny Cavendish, also known as Stoker, is the 12th Duke of Devonshire whose main residence continues to be Chatsworth House, Derbyshire, England, having been passed down through 16 generations of the Cavendish family since Bess.

Acknowledgements

This may seem a cliché but without the support and encouragement from incredible family and friends this book would not have been possible, I'm one very lucky lady and really do count my blessings to have you all in my life. Thank you to Lynne, Chris, Mike, Ken, Elena, James, Leon, Melissa, Charlotte, Lynn, Julie, Zoe, Bruce and my big bro' Phil for your positivity, encouragement and of course your advice, always appreciated.

Thanks to Bretton, Jenny, Tyler and Howard for your encouragement and to Pete for listening to me droning on about this venture, I know you've 'switched off' more than a few times! Special thanks to Corey for putting up with my many, many book covering variants as I was redesigning them and also to you for coming up with my next book cover by mistake! To Mum and Dad, I cannot thank you enough for your positivity, encouragement, love and support.

To my Publishers AuthorHouse UK, the Design, Editing, Printing and Marketing Teams and especially Homer and May for your continued professionalism, advice, patience and being there for me, but most of all for seeing the potential and believing in myself and my books, I look forward to our future book ventures together.

And finally, to you, thank you for giving me a chance by reading my book. I hope you continue to enjoy the journey with me and enjoy my other books in this my 'in simple terms' collection just as much as this one.

Appendices

The material contained in this book has been obtained using various sources, placed into words and written with the purpose of information only, with just enough scope to whet your reader appetite in order to find out more about Bess, her descendants and Hardwick Hall itself.

Hardwick Hall was the last property and final home Bess had constructed, with the assumption that her grandaughter, who lived with her, Lady Arbella Stuart, would be named the next Monarch of England by Queen Elizabeth I, therefore this home had to be of a status standard, indeed a house fit for a Princess.

The New Hall, as it is also known, has been part of the National Trust since 1959. Prior to that Hardwick Hall was still used and lived in by the Cavendish family.

There are still ruins of the Old Hall and birth place of Bess only a few yards away from the New Hall. The Old Hall is part of the Registered Charity English Heritage.

I hope you enjoyed reading or listening to my book as much as I enjoyed researching and writing it.

Why not come along and visit Hardwick Hall and Gardens, you will not be disappointed.

About The Author

Alison lives in South Yorkshire, England. She has 3 sons, one grandson and 2 dogs. She is an in-house Day Leader/ Volunteers Manager on Sunday's and Bank Holiday Monday's at Hardwick Hall, a 420+ year old stately home in Derbyshire, now run by the National Trust. The Hall continues to inspire and intrigue her and has done so for as long as she can remember. She is part of the Learning Team both on and off-site and was involved in volunteer teaching students on/offsite for part of the AQA GCSE History exam for UK Secondary Schools in 2018. She is also a volunteer room guide in the Hall. Alison attends various group meetings off-site and online to give personal talks about Bess of Hardwick, Bess's family and descendants, the history of Hardwick Hall inside/outside and some of the various collections in the Hall. She's always had a fascination with History but maybe she loves chocolate more – you'd have to ask her!

Alison can be contacted at aliwilm24@yahoo.com
Or via Facebook Page… In Simple Terms Book
Collection by Alison Ratcliffe-Williams
Or via Instagram Page… aliwilm24_author